Thomas Grantham

An Historical Account of Some Memorable Actions

Particularly in Virginia

Also against the Admiral of Algier, and in the East Indies: performed for

the service of his prince and country

Thomas Grantham

An Historical Account of Some Memorable Actions Particularly in Virginia
Also against the Admiral of Algier, and in the East Indies: performed for the service of his prince and country

ISBN/EAN: 9783337319175

Printed in Europe, USA, Canada, Australia, Japan

Cover: Foto ©ninafisch / pixelio.de

More available books at **www.hansebooks.com**

AN

Historical Account

OF SOME

MEMORABLE ACTIONS,

Particularly in Virginia;

ALSO

Against the Admiral of Algier, and in the
East Indies: Performed for the Service of his Prince and Country,

BY SIR THOMAS GRANTHAM, KNIGHT,

WITH AN INTRODUCTION

BY R. A. BROCK, ESQUIRE,

Secretary Virginia Historical Society.

PREFACE.

At a meeting of the Joint Library Committee of the Legislature of Virginia, held February 18, 1882, Colonel SHERWIN McRAE, the Librarian, presented the following report concerning the book now reprinted:

"The volume containing 'THE MEMORABLE ACTIONS OF SIR THOMAS GRANTHAM, PARTICULARLY IN VIRGINIA,' is for the Library a most fortunate acquisition; throwing much light, as it does, on a part of the history of Virginia on which historians and scholars differ. This merit alone would demand its purchase, but in addition, there is good reason to believe that this copy which the Library possesses is the only one in existence. This fact (if so), independently of the intrinsic worth of the book, greatly increases its money value."

After the reading of the above, the Committee heard the application of the publisher for the privilege of reprinting, and unanimously passed the following resolution, which limits the edition to one hundred copies; but as the minutes were not written immediately, the Secretary has failed to note that the publisher was allowed discre-

tion in that matter, to the extent necessary to secure
himself from loss:

"Leave was granted Mr. Carlton McCarthy to take from the
Library the rare book entitled 'THE MEMORABLE ACTIONS OF
SIR THOMAS GRANTHAM, 1716,' and to print therefrom one
hundred copies, upon condition that he return the book in
good order, and give the Library ten of the copies so printed."

True copy from Journal of Joint Library Committee, February
18, 1882.

SHERWIN McRAE,

Assistant and Acting Librarian.

INTRODUCTION.

The original of the little tract, which is herewith for the first time reprinted, is in the Library of the State of Virginia, for which it was recently purchased in the city of New York. Upon the tract the critical bibliographer Sabin thus comments: "A very rare piece. I have only seen one copy." (Dictionary of Books relating to America, No. 28,323.) It is the judgment of Colonel Sherwin McRae, the State Librarian, who has given the matter careful investigation, that the copy in his custody and that noted by Sabin are one and the same, and that it is in all probability the only copy in America. The tract is mentioned by Lowndes (Manual of Bibliography), who ascribes to the same author, also, "The Prisoner against the Prelate, or a Dialogue between the Common Gaol and the Cathedral of London, 1650. 8vo."

Allibone (Dictionary of Authors) gives the following only as the productions of Sir Thomas Grantham: "The Prisoner against the Prelate, 1650; Christianismus and Primivitus, 1678, folio; other theological works, 1644—80." The present tract, aside from its rarity, is of interest and value in the novel details which it furnishes of one of the most memorable episodes in the early history of Virginia—that popular uprising known as Bacon's Rebellion.

The leader in this movement was Nathaniel Bacon, Jr., a member of the distinguished English family of the name, and whose life gave no uncertain assurance of his noble heritage.

Scarcely thirty years of age, possessed of ample fortune, learned, eloquent, invested with the honorable station of Councillor, popular with all classes, a happy husband and father, his patriotism and philanthropy cannot justly be questioned. He had all to lose and nothing to gain by opposing the existing authorities. His oratorical powers are strikingly evidenced in the lofty declaration quoted in the tract (pp. 12, 13), which is a noble vindication, as well, of the purity of his motives.

Virginia groaned beneath the accumulated oppressions of Charles the Second and his insatiate minions. The profligate monarch found a fitting viceroy in the choleric and uncompromising Berkeley, who gives infamous testimony to his own character in his memorable reply to an inquiry of the English Council: "I thank God there are no free-schools, nor printing, and I hope we shall not have these three hundred years; for learning has brought disobedience into the world, and printing has divulged them and libels against the best government. God keep us from both!"*

To the intolerable grievances of the Colonists, was added another, imminently vital, in their defenceless surrender by the Governor to Indian massacre. Denied protection by him, they had no recourse but in revolt. They found a leader in Bacon, who had an immediate stimulant in the murder by the savages of his overseer and a favorite servant, at his plantation near Richmond, on the stream still known as Bacon Quarter Branch.

---

* Hening's Statutes at Large, vol. ii, p. 511.

Bacon, having subdued the savages and convoked an Assembly (which by enactment reformed many abuses), suddenly died from disease occasioned by exposure—supreme in the affections of the people, and in the plenitude of his power.

With the death of their gifted and heroic leader, and the threatened approach of a force sent from England for their reduction, the rebellion subsided and the insurgents dispersed, to be hunted down and relentlessly punished by the vindictive Berkeley. The prisons were filled with the unfortunate patriots, their estates were confiscated, and twenty-three were executed. The virulence of Berkeley seemed to gather strength with each execution, and it was urged of him that he "would have hanged half the country if they had let him alone."* At last, the Assembly interposed to arrest his blood-thirsty vengeance, at the extent of which, even his selfish and hypocritical master, Charles the Second, was horror-stricken, and was heard to say "that old fool had hanged more men in that naked country than he had done for the murder of his father."†

For details of Bacon's Rebellion, the reader is referred to the following original narratives in Force's Tracts, vol. i:

The Beginning, Progress, and Conclusion of Bacon's Rebellion in Virginia in the year 1675 and 1676. Washington: Printed by Peter Force. 1835. Pp. 26.

An Account of Our Late Troubles in Virginia, written in 1676, by Mrs. An. Cotton, of Q. Creeke. Published from the original manuscript, in the Richmond (Va.) Enquirer, of 12 September, 1804. Washington: Printed by Peter Force. 1835. Pp. 12.

---

* T. M.'s Account in Force's Tracts, vol. i, p. 24; Burke, vol. ii, p. 208.   † Ibid.

A List of those that have been Executed for the Late Rebellion in Virginia, by Sir William Berkeley, Governor of the Colony. Copied from the original manuscript (Harleian collection, codex 6845, page 54) in the library of the British Museum, London, by Robert Greenhow, Esq., of Virginia. Washington: Printed by Peter Force. 1835. Pp. 4.

A Narrative of the Indian and Civil Wars in Virginia, in years 1675 and 1676. Published from the original manuscript in the first volume (second series) of the Collections of the Massachusetts Historical Society. Boston: Printed by John Elliott, No. 5 Court street. 1814. Pp. 48. (This manuscript is now in the Collections of the Virginia Historical Society.)

See also Hening's Statutes, vol. ii; Collections of the Massachusetts Historical Society, vol. ix, 4th series (Aspinwall Papers), pp. 162–187; Bancroft's History of the United States; and the several histories of Virginia.

There are also in the State Library of Virginia, copious extracts from the Public Record Office of Great Britain, relating to the period, furnished by W. Noël Sainsbury, Esq.

R. A. BROCK.

RICHMOND, *March 7, 1882.*

An HISTORICAL

ACCOUNT

OF SOME

Memorable Actions,

Particularly in VIRGINIA;

ALSO

Againſt the Admiral of *Algier*,
and in the *Eaſt Indies*:

Perform'd for the Service of his
Prince and *Country*,

BY

Sʳ *Thomas Grantham*, Kᵗ

---

*The Winning of Honour, is but the Revealing of Man's
Virtue and Worth, without Diſadvantage.*
Bac. Eſſays.

L O N D O N:

Printed for J. ROBERTS, near the *Oxford-Arms*
in *Warwick-Lane*. MDCCXVI.

THE

Memorable Actions

OF

Sr *Thomas Grantham.*

S the Dictates of Nature are of Force sufficient for securing the Safety of Particular Beings, and available enough, without the Assistance of any other Motives, for Self-Defence and Preservation: So the Ties we are under, from the Relation which we bear to Communities, and as we all are link'd together in Society, engage our Care for their Defence, and our Concern for their Welfare. Both the Country where we Live, and the Prince that does Protect us, claim from us a particular Regard for their Interest

and

and Happinefs; which if we neglect, as far as we are able, to promote; we neceffarily fall fhort of our Duty, and those Civil Obligations, to which the Laws of Obedience and Loyalty, and of Society engage us.

Upon which Account it was, that I here have undertaken to publifh fome of thofe Tranfactions, which a long Time have lain dormant; and which could not eafily be kept filent, without a fhameful Neglect, both of the Favours Sir *Thomas Grantham* receiv'd from the Bounty of his Sovereign, for the Service perform'd in his Plantation of *Virginia*; and alfo of the Generous Returns made to him by the Honourable Company of Merchants Trading to the *Eaft-Indies*, for his Conduct and Succefs in Reducing of *Bombay*. For tho' the private Satisfaction that flows from every worthy Deed, is a Recompence endearing to each Brave and Honeft Mind; yet the Benevolence they fhowed to thefe Publick Undertakings, was an additional Reward to the unfeen inward Delight, and made the Actions pregnant with a Treble Happinefs of Pleafure, and of Profit and Renown; as will appear by the following Hiftory and Account.

In

In the Year, therefore, 1672, Sir *Thomas* being bound on a Voyage for *Virginia*, as Captain of the Ship *Edward and Jane*, he obtain'd from his Royal Highnefs the Duke of *York*, Protection for fome of his Men: Of which this is the Copy.

JAMES Duke of *York* and *Albany*, Earl of *Ulſter*, Lord High-Admiral of *ENGLAND* and *IRELAND*, Conſtable of *Dover*-Caſtle, Lord Warden of the *Cinque-Ports*, and Governor of *Portsmouth*, &c.

*Y*OU *are not to Imprefs into His Maje-ſty's Service, any of the Twelve Men hereunder nam'd belonging to the Ship* Edward *and* Jane, *Burthen about* 240 *Tons, whereof* Thomas Grantham, *One of my Guard, is Commander; which is bound on a Voyage to* Virginia. *Given under my Hand and Seal, on Board the*

the Prince, *this* 25th *of* J U N E , 1672.

To all Commanders of His Majesty's
Shipes, and all Others whom it
may concern.

J A M E S.

But, after this, having One of his Men imprest by a Fireship, he obtain'd his Release, by an Order from Prince *Rupert;* which is as follows.

Prince *RUPERT*, Count *Palatine* of the *Rhine*, Duke of *Bavaria* and *Cumberland*, Vice-Admiral of *England*, and Governor of the Royal Castle and Honour of *Windsor*, &c.

*B*Y *Virtue of the Power and Authority to Me given by His Royal Highness the Duke of* York, *and confirmed by His Majesty, These are to require you forthwith to Discharge* George Robins, *belonging to the Ship* Edward *and* Jane *of* London, *whereof* Thomas Grantham *is Commander, bound on a Voyage to* Virginia *for His Majesty's*

*jesty's Service; whom you have lately im-
pres'd. Hereof you are not to fail. Given
under my Hand* and *Seal at* Whitehall, *the*
5*th Day of* August, 1672.

To the Commander of His Majesty's   R U P E R T.
Fire-Ship the Truelove.

Upon this he proceeded, by the Bles-
sing of God, on his intended Voyage:
And having happily arriv'd, after some
Time, at *Virginia;* he addres'd himself
to the Governor thereof, Sir *William
Berkley,* who receiv'd him with several
Marks of Friendship and Esteem; and as
a Token of the great Confidence he had
in his Fidelity and Valour, he appointed
him Admiral of a Fleet of Ships, consist-
ing of 25 Sail, for their Safe and Prospe-
rous Conduct Home: His Majesty being
then engag'd in a dangerous and bloody
War with the *States-General* of the *United
Provinces.*

In the Time of this Sir *William,* it
was, that *Oliver* subdued the Colony of
Virginia: Tho', to the immortal Honour
of the Loyalty of the Place, it was the
last of all the King's Dominions, that submitted to the Usurpation, and the first
that

that caſt it off. For the Governor caus'd the King to be proclaim'd there, before he return'd for *England*. The Commiſſion he gave Sir *Thomas* then, was this: *Viz.*

By the Governor, and Captain-General of *Virginia*.

*W*Hereas I have receiv'd Command from his moſt Sacred Majeſty, in his Royal Letters dated the 10th of March, in the 24th year of His Majeſty's Reign, That during theſe Times of Danger, occaſion'd by this preſent War with the States-General of the United Provinces, I ſhould not permit any Ships to depart from hence, but on the 24th of March, June, and September; and that during their Stay here, and their Voyage home, I ſhould appoint ſome of the Ableſt Commanders, to Order and Direct the Fleet under their Charge, until ſuch Time as they ſhall either meet with ſome of His Majeſty's Ships of War in the Soundings, or ſhall arrive in ſome Port of England, there to expect further Orders. Now, know you all, whom theſe under may concern; that I, Sir William Berkley, Kt. Governor, and Captain-Gene-*
                                                                 ral

ral of Virginia, *out of the Confidence I
have in the Valour and good Conduct of
you,* Captain Thomas Grantham, *do hereby, according to His Majesty's Commands,
and the Power thereof, constitute and appoint you Admiral of the Fleet now to
Sail; hereby giving you full Power and
Authority, as Admiral, to Command the
said Fleet; in His Majesty's Name requiring you to obey ond observe such Orders and
Instructions, as I shall give you. And I
do hereby straitly command and require all
inferior Officers, and Masters of Ships and
Vessels now to Sail, to be from time to time
obedient to you, as Admiral; and so far
as the Wind and Weather will permit them,
to observe such Orders, as shall by you and
your Inferior Officers be thought fit for your
greatest Security, and are according to His
Majesty's Commands, and my Instructions,
grounded thereon; as you, and they, and
every of them, will answer the contrary
to His Majesty, and upon the Forfeiture
of your several Bonds. Given under my
Hand, and the Seal of the Colony, this* 2d
Day of April, 1673.

William Berkley.

B Arri-

Arriving therefore in *England* in good time, with the Ships under his Care, he embark'd again in the Year 1676. for *Virginia*, in the Ship *Concord*, Burthen 500 Tonns, with near 50 Men. The Name of the Ship feem'd to be given providentially, and as an Omen of that peaceable and friendly Settlement, to which the Country was reduc'd by his prevailing Mediation. For Civil Faction and Rebellion was fo far advanc'd when he came there, that a Subverfion of the Government was very dangeroufly threatned, and the Incendiaries were grown to fuch a Pitch of Mutiny and Difturbance, that nothing could either allay, or appeafe them.

Their Reftless Tempers were inflam'd on thefe Accounts: *Viz.* The Difturbance of the *Indians*; the Reftraint of their Trade by *Englifh* Acts of Parliament; the ill Ufage the Planters met with in Exchange of their Tobacco for other Commodities; and the Dividing the Colony into Proprieties, contrary to the Original Charters; and the Charges of Relieving themfelves from thofe Grants. Which various Complaints Colonel *Nathaniel Bacon* obferving, he thereupon

infi-

infinuated himfelf into the Affections of the Difcontented; and fends for a Commiffion to the Governor to head the Men againft the *Indians*. But the Governor refus'd it; and order'd him to be proclaim'd a Rebel, if he refus'd to come to him. After this, *Bacon* came with 600 Men arm'd; and the Governor not finding himfelf powerful enough to refift him, fign'd his Commiffion; but as soon as he was gone, iffued out a Proclamation of Rebellion againft him. Whereupon *Bacon* and his Men, inftead of Marching againft the *Indians*, turn'd their Arms againft fuch of their own Country as fhould oppofe them. Their Demands were fo infulting, and their Pretenfions fo exorbitant, that neither Reafon could mitigate, nor Authority curb them.

Bacon, therefore, and *Lawrence*, were the chief Ringleaders of this Tumult and Difturbance; and they, with the reft of their daring Accomplices, forc'd the Governor, and moft of the Council and Principal Inhabitants, to fly for Safety to a Place call'd *Accomack*, on the *North* Side of *Cape-Henry*.

Nathaniel Bacon publifh'd Two Declarations; one to the People of *Accomack*, and the other to thofe of *Virginia*; in-

citing

citing both of them to an open Infurre-
ction.

In the Firſt, He animates the People to
a High Refentment of thofe Grievous
Oppreſſions they lay under from the Government of Sir *William Berkley*; becaufe
he acted beyond his Power and Commiſ-
fion; and that they had been fuccefsful
in their War againſt him. In the Second,
to the Inhabitants of *Virginia*, he begins
with this High Strain of his Innocence,
and the Juſtice of their Caufe.

" If Virtue be a Sin; if Piety be
"Guilt; if all the Principles of Morali-
"ty, and Goodnefs, and Juſtice be per-
"verted; we muſt confefs, that thofe
"who are call'd Rebels, may be in Dan-
"ger of thofe high Imputations, thofe
"loud and fevere Bulls, which would af-
"fright Innocency, and render the De-
"fence of our Brethren, and the Enquiry
"into our fad and heavy Oppreſſions,
"Treafon. But if there be (as fure there
"is) a juſt God to appeal to; if Religion
"and Juſtice be a Sanctuary here; if
"to plead the Caufe of the Opprefs'd; if
"fincerely to aim at the Publick Good,
"without any Refervation, or By-Intereſt;
"if to ſtand in the Gap, after fo much
                                    " Blood

"Blood of our Dear Brethren bought and
"fold; if after the Lofs of a great Part of
"His Majefty's Colony, deferted and dif-
"peopl'd, and freely to part with our
"Lives and Eftates, to endeavour to fave
"the Remainder, be Treafon; Let God
"and the World judge, and the Guilty
"die. But fince we cannot find in our
"Hearts One fingle Spot of Rebellion and
"Treafon, or that we have in any man-
"ner aim'd at the Subverfion of the Set-
"tl'd Government, or attempting the
"Perfon of any, either Magiftrate, or
"Private Man; notwithftanding the fe-
"veral Reproaches and Threats of fome,
"who for finifter Ends were difaffected to
"Us, and cenfure our Juft and Honeft
"Defigns.—— Let Truth be bold; and
"all the World know the Real Foundation
"of our Pretended Guilt.

After this, he taxes the Governor, Sir
William, with Caballing, and Myfterious
Defigns; with Promoting the *Indians* to
Employments, the Neglect of Trade, and
of the Arts and Sciences. And accufes
him for Expending the Publick Treafure
upon his Favourites; for Protecting the
Indians, who are Enemies to the King and
Country, and are Thieves and Robbers,
and

and have Ammunition and Fire-Arms allow'd them, contrary to Law: And that he himfelf had monopoliz'd the Beaver Trade, in Oppofition to the Settlement.

And then concludes, That he, and his Adherents, unanimoufly defire to prefent their fad and heavy Grievances to His moft Sacred Majefty, and Parliament of *England*, as their Refuge and Sanctuary; where they know, that all their Caufes will be impartially heard, and equal Juftice adminiftred to all People.

And whereas the Rebels continu'd their Trade in Tobacco, notwithftanding the Laws of the Colony to the contrary, and the Governor's Publick Prohibitions; the faid Governor therefore order'd this Proclamation following to be publifh'd.

By the Governor, and Captain-General of *Virginia*.

*W*Hereas *I have heretofore iffu'd forth, and publifh'd feveral Proclamations, thereby ftrictly forbidding all Perfons what-foever, as well Mafters of Ships, Mariners, Merchants, as Factors refiding in* *this*

this Countrey, and such as come this Year into this Countrey, as Others, from all manner of Trading, or Dealing in any sort with those in Rebellion; which Proclamations and Prohibitions have not hitherto been directly observed: But that on the contrary, several Persons have dispos'd of Goods on Shore, purchas'd Tobacco to considerable Quantities, and procur'd several Hogsheads of Tobacco to be put on Board several Ships; whereby the Rebels are encourag'd, and enabl'd to persist and continue in Rebellion against his Loyal and Liege People, greatly prejudic'd and dishearten'd in their Estates and Loyalty; for that those in Rebellion and Wavering from their Allegiance, have by that means the sole Opportunty of Serving themselves in the Disposal and Securing their Tobacco, and Furnishing themselves with Goods and Necessaries; whilst those truly Loyal are forc'd from their Houses and Plantations, and their Estates seized, robb'd, and taken away. All which such Trading, Dealing, or Handling, is directly prejudicial to the King's most Sacred Majesty's Country, and is in it self Rebellious and Traiterous.

I do

I do therefore this once more, by this my Proclamation, not only reinforce my former Proclamations, prohibiting all such Trade; but again strictly forbid all Persons whatsoever, from any such Trading or Dealing whatsoever, with any Persons on the Western *Shore in* Virginia, *and also from Receiving any Tobacco on Shore, or Taking any Tobacco whatsoever on Board any Ship, or other Vessel, in order to be transported out of this Country, during the Continuance of this Rebellion, except by my especial Leave and License in Writing, under my Hand for the same; upon the Pains and Penalties of being deem'd, held and esteem'd, as Rebels and Traytors to His most Sacred Majesty; for that the same is of Necessity a Nursing, Maintaining, and Strengthening the Rebellion on foot. Given under my Hand in* York River, *this* 25th *Day of* December 1676. *and in the* 28th *Year of the Reign of our Sovereign Lord King* Charles *the* IId. *whom God preserve.*

WILLIAM BERKLEY.

To all Magistrates and Officers Civil and Military, and all other His Majesty's Liege People; who are strictly Commanded to Publish the same by this Original, or a true Copy thereof.

This

This the Governor thought neceſſary for Reducing the Rebels to some Exigences and Straits, and thereby to hearken more eaſily to Terms of Peace and Accommodation.

In the Time of the Rebellion, Sir *Thomas* receiv'd a Letter from Mr. *Richard Lawrence*, One of the Rebels, to this Effect. ' That the Good Subjects of *Virgi-* ' *nia* (as he call'd them; tho' then they ' were in open Rebellion) were grievouſly ' oppreſſ'd, and had taken up Arms for ' their own Defence, and that of His Ma- ' jeſty's Plantation. And deſir'd, that he ' would not condemn them as guilty of ' the horrid Crimes of Treaſon and Rebel- ' lion, which they from their very Souls ' abhorr'd more than their Enemies. He urg'd to him likewise, ' That the Gover- ' nor's Commiſſion was expir'd, and void- ' ed by his own Act: And that if He, ' and the reſt of the Commanders of ' Ships, would not ſtand *Neuter*, they ' would burn all the Tobacco, as they ' had formerly done: And that the Burn- ' ing of the present Crop, would heighten ' the Value of the next.

To this Letter, he immediately return'd this Anſwer. 'That nothing but a ſpeedy
' Repentance could free him, and his
' Friends, and the Country from inevita-
' ble Ruin: Which the Governor was ve-
' ry willing to prevent, by extending to
' them his Mercy, as far as it was confi-
' ſtent with his Honour and Safety. And
' that his Commiſſion was so far from be-
' ing expir'd, that the King was Extending
' his Power, and Sending him more large
' Inſtructions. That as for himself, and
' the reſt of the Commanders, they durſt
' not disobey the Governor's Commands,
' left they ſhould incur the high Diſplea-
' ſure of his Majeſty at their Return; who
' would alſo doubtleſs be very much in-
' cens'd at the Loſſ of his Cuſtoms, by
' their Impoveriſhing the Country; and
' the Merchants also, by the Loſs of their
' Trade, would unanimouſly follicit the
' Puniſhment of all thoſe, who were the
' turbulent Promoters of it. And at laſt
ſubſcrib'd himſelf,

Your very Loving Friend,

(*As far as my Allegiance to my
King, and my Duty to my Governor will permit,*)

Tho. Grantham.

And

And therefore, as he was not unmindful of his Duty to his Prince, so neither was he forgetful of that Kindness which he ow'd his Fellow-Subjects: And therefore employ'd his most sedulous Care and Interest, to promote that Tranquility and Good Understanding betwixt the Governor and the Rebels, that the Country, and its Inhabitants, might not be brought to utter Misery and Desolation. Nor could he think of any Method more conducive towards the Accomplishing this Good Design, than to perswade the Governor to Meekness, and the People to Submission. For, as an unrelenting Temper in Sir *William*, would be apt to harden them in their Obstinacy, and render them desperate, while they thought their Crimes unpardonable; so their Inclination of Hearkning to any Amicable Proposals, would be apt to soften the Governor into Kindness, and asswage his Anger and Resentment. And therefore, he perswaded them not to be led away by Evil Counsellors, nor to run the Hazard of Destroying both their Souls, and Bodies, and Estates; which are the common and most dire Effects of Sedition and Rebellion.

For

For, after his Arrival in *York*-River, he immediately went to *Portopatank*, where he heard the Rebels were affembled; and near Mr. *Pate's* Houfe he met with the principal Ringleaders, to whom he addrefs'd himfelf to this Effect. ' What, ' Gentlemen, are you going to your Ruin ' headlong? Are you quite bereft of all ' Senfe of Duty, and Self-Prefervation? ' Have neither the Staple Laws of Na- ' ture, nor thofe Fundamental Rules of ' your Country, any Influence upon you; ' that your Obftinacy thus blinds you? ' Have you not yet heard what numerous ' Forces are coming from *England*, to fup- ' prefs your tumultuous Proceedings? And ' that without an immediate Submiffion, ' your Fate will be inevitable, and your ' Safety entirely fhipwreck'd? Hearken ' therefore to the Tenders of Peace, be- ' fore it is too late: Confult, like Men of ' Senfe, your own Felicity; and quietly ' lay down your Arms; left by perfifting ' in this open Hoftility, you force them at ' laft to be fheath'd in your own Bow- ' els.

And by the Bleffing of God upon this Advice, which was attended with fome fevere Threats, the Civil Breach was clos'd

be-

between them, and the Animosities at last expir'd.

About this Time, he receiv'd a kind and sensible Letter from Mr. *Milner;* which, because it is not long, shall be transcrib'd.

SIR,

YOU have undertaken a Work, that will speak your everlasting Fame and Glory; the Consolidating our sad Differences, Preventing the Sword and Famine, with other Horrors, that, gaping, were ready to swallow up this miserable Country. The Service you will do herein to the Almighty, to our Dread Sovereign, the Governor, and the Country, will make you honourably spoken of throughout the World. I have only to add, that since now, as I hope, it will appear by the whole Series of my Actions, my Life and Fortune are both Shipp'd off with the Governor and his Friends; if therefore I may be thought worthy to advise, I shall leave to your serious Consideration; That, if you think good, the Honourable Governor be perswaded to proceed by the same Method His Majesty did at his Restoration, by a Declaration from Bredagh. *Such a one here from his Honour, would*

abun-

abundantly settle the Minds of Hundreds, that are at present amus'd, and at a full Stand. All I add is, That Mercy and Indemnity were ever yet a greater Friend to Peace, than Severity, tho' Justice were on the same Side. I beseech you to dispatch the Bearer back, lest I am forc'd to come single, and then render my self incapable of doing that Service to the Honourable Governor, which is design'd by

Your Faithful Servant,

Jan. 6. 1676.

Geo. Milner.

The Governor was pleas'd to manage his Proceedings, according to the Rules of this Advice. And therefore, tho' some of those who animated the Faction were put to Death; and *Bacon* died of the Lousy Evil; yet others, who submitted themselves, were receiv'd into Favour and Protection. And to these the following Oath of Allegiance and Fidelity was administred by Sir *Thomas.*

' I *A. B.* do willingly and heartily de-
' clare, that I know, and in my Confci-
' ence believe, *Richard Lawrence*, and
' many others with him, to be in open Re-
' bellion againſt the King's moſt Sacred
' Majeſty, and againſt the Right Honou-
' rable the Governor of *Virginia*, and the
' good eſtabliſh'd Laws and Peace of this
' Colony of *Virginia*. Which Rebellion
' I do from my Heart abhor and deteſt,
' and do therefore moſt willingly, freely,
' and from my Heart ſwear my full Alle-
' giance to the King's moſt Excellent Ma-
' jeſty; and that I will with my Life, and
' whole Eſtate, ſerve and obey the Right
' Honourable the Governor, and obey all
' ſuch Magiſtrates and Officers, as he ſhall
' from time to time appoint over me; and
' with them, or any of them, uſe my ut-
' moſt Endeavour to my Life's End, to
' take, ſeize, kill and deſtroy, all ſuch
' Perſons whatsoever, as either now are,
' or hereafter ſhall be in such Rebellion as
' is recited. This Oath I do moſt hearti-
' ly, freely, and willingly take, in the
' Preſence of Almighty God. So help me
God.

When

When all thefe Uproars were at an end, and the Government fettl'd on its old Bafis of Tranquility and Peace, he return'd for *England;* and acquainted His Majefty with the welcome News of Reducing the Rebels to their Duty, and Fixing the Governor in his Power and Command. All which was perform'd with no lefs Management, than apparent Hazard of his Life. For which Signal Service, His Majefty was gracioufly pleas'd to beftow upon him a Noble Gift, as a Token of his Princely Kindnefs to his Loyalty and Good Offices.

In the Year 1676, he proceeded again on on a Voyage to *Virginia,* in the fame Ship *Concord,* with about 50 Men, including Paffengers, and only 22 Guns. And failing forward to about 120 Leagues beyond the Land's-End, was attack'd by one *Canary,* a *Spanifh* Renegado, and Admiral of the King of *Algiers,* in a New Ship of 48 Guns call'd the *New Rofe,* and having on Board more than 600 Men. From whence afterwards arofe the *English* Proverb of a *Canary-Bird,* fignifying a Rogue. His Bravery for the Defence of his Ship, was as remarkable, as his Perfidioufnefs had been to the Christian Faith: And it was

his

his Courage and Refolution that gain'd him that High Poft in his Earthly Mafter's Service, whatever Cowardice and Means he had betray'd unto his Heavenly.

This Fight happen'd upon *Thurfday* the 25th of *October;* which was extreme defperate and bloody on both Sides. When they came up with one another, *Canary* hal'd him; and pretending to be his Friend, told him the Name of his Ship was the *Rupert.* He anfwer'd him, He did not believe him. *Canary* then commanded him to hoift out his Boat, and come on Board: Which he refus'd; and bad him come on Board him; which he told him he would do fpeedily. This being in the Evening, he prepar'd himfelf for a Fight the next Morning. At which Time hoifting his Top-Sails, he came up to Sir *Thomas,* on his Larboard-Quarter; and letting fly a Red Swallow-Tail Flag at Main-Top-Maft-Head, he fir'd a Shot at him, and commanded him to ftrike to the King of *Algiers,* and Admiral *Canary;* Which he refufing, he came along his Broad Side, and fir'd his Great Guns at him, with a Volley of Small Shot. He return'd him the like Salute. And this was done twice on both Sides. After this

D   he

he grappl'd with Sir *Thomas* his Mizon-
Chains, fir'd his Great Guns, and mann'd
his Decks, and put him to a clofe Fight.
But in two Hours time, by God's Affiftance, Sir *Thomas* beat him off twice or
thrice. He fhot down the Mizon-Yard,
fir'd the Mizon-Sail, burnt down the Mi-
zon-Maft, and putting all abaft on Fire,
Sir *Thomas* was forc'd down into the great
Cabin, when every Man in that Quarter
was either kill'd or wounded, but himfelf;
refolving rather to burn, than to be taken.

From the great Cabin, Sir *Thomas*
made a Sign to thofe in the Fore-Caftle,
to Sally out at the fame time with him;
whereby they kill'd feveral, and forc'd
others into the Sea, and aboard their Ship.
He then endeavour'd to get away; but
having faften'd his Spritfail Top-Maft to
Sir *Thomas's* Main-Bowling-Bridle, he
kept him faft: And as often as he fent up
his Men, One by One, to the Boltfprit to
get clear, Sir *Thomas* his Men fhot them
down; and prevented alfo his extinguifh-
ing his Fore-yard, which hung over Sir
Thomas his Ship's Poop, all on Fire. But
at laft his Fore-Sail, Mafts and Yards being all in a Light Flame, he was cut loofe,
and

and about Twelve at Noon they parted.
Sir *Thomas* ſtood after him till it was
dark, but was not unwilling to loſe Sight
of him notwithſtanding. In this Fight,
Sir *Thomas* had 21 Seamen and Paſſengers
kill'd and wounded.

And, after this, making a Safe Voyage
Outward, and Home, he related the whole
Matter to the King; who, in Conſideration of ſo Noble an Exploit, rewarded
him according to his Royal Bounty, with
a very Valuable Gold Chain and Medal.
Nor were the Owners of the Ship unmindful of this Proof of his Ability and
Conduct; and therefore they agreed to
make this following Order.

Mr. K E N T,

WE, *the Owners of the Ship* Concord, *do agree, and order you, in
Conſideration of the extraordinary Ma-
naging the Fight againſt the* Turks, *this
laſt Voyage by Captain* Grantham, *to lay
out, and buy Plate to the Value of Forty Pounds. Which Plate is to be engra-
ven with Two* Turks *Heads, and written,* The Gift of the ſaid Owners:
Which are to be carried in the ſaid Ship,

D 2 *as*

*as long as the Captain goes to Sea. Sub-
fcrib'd by Us this 27th of* Auguft,
1679.

For RICHARD BOOTH *and Self,*

SAMUEL STORY.

For JOHN LENTON *and Self,*

FRAN. KEMPE.

ARTHUR BAILEY.

MATT. MERITON.

GEORGE BAKER.

THURST. WITHNELL.

The Relation of this Engagement was
alfo publifh'd in the *Gazette,* Thurfday,
December 5th. 1678.

Nor were thefe Remarkable Inftances of
Bounty the fole Reward he receiv'd from
His Majefty and the Owners; but the
King was likewife pleas'd to appoint him
Keeper of his *Busby*-Park. And what was
kinder, as a Teftimony of his Special Fa-
vour, he recommended him by a Special
Mandate, under the Signet and Sign Ma-
nual, to the Governor and Company of
Mer-

Merchants Trading to the *Eaſt-Indies.* It run thus.

Charles R.

*T*Ruſty, *and Well-beloved, we greet you well. Whereas our Truſty and Well-beloved Captain* Thomas Grantham *has given Eminent Proofs of his abſo-lute Courage and Loyalty upon ſeveral Occaſions, which deſerve to receive all fitting Encouragement: We have thought fit, as a Mark of our Favour to him, hereby to recommend him in a moſt par-ticular manner to you; that he, and his Ship which he intends to build, may be enter-tain'd by you, according to your uſual Pra-ctice in your Trade to the* Eaſt-Indies. *And ſo not doubting of your ready Compliance herein, which we ſhall take in very good*

part,

part, We bid you Farewel. Given at our Court at Whitehall, *the Third Day of* March, 168½. *in the Four and Twentieth Year of our Reign.*

By His Majesty's Command,

C O N W A Y.

After the Ship was built and finish'd, Burthen 816 Ton, and carrying 300 Men, His Majesty, with his Royal Highness the Duke of *York*, and several of the Principal Nobility, did him the Honour of Coming Aboard on Her at *Deptford*, and receiv'd from him an Entertainment. And His Majesty having at that time nam'd the Ship *Charles the Second*, conferr'd upon him the Honour of Knighthood, *Feb.* 18. 168⅔.

After this he receiv'd his Orders from the *East-India* Company; which were these.

Com-

Commiſſion and Inſtructions, given by the Governor and Company of Merchants of London, *Trading to the* Eaſt-Indies; *to Sir* Thomas Gratham, *Kt. Commander of the Ship* Charles the Second.

'THE King's moſt Excellent Maje-
' ſty having, by his Royal Charter
' bearing Date the 3d. of *April*, 1661. in
' the Thirteenth Year of His Majeſty's
' Reign, granted unto us the Entire Trade
' of the *Eaſt-Indies*, and declar'd, that the
' Ports, Cities, Towns and Places thereof,
' ſhall not be traded unto, viſited, fre-
' quented, or haunted by any other of
' His Majeſty's Subjects, without our Li-
' cence; upon Pain of Forfeiture of Ship,
' Goods, and Impriſonment during His
' Majeſty's Pleaſure. And that if we con-
' ceive it neceſſary, we may ſend either
' Ships of War, Men, or Ammunition in-
' to any of our Factories, or other Places
' of Trade, for the Security and Defence
' of the ſame: and to chuſe Commanders
                                                    ' and

' and Officers over them; and to give them
' Power and Authority, by Commiſſion
' under our Common Seal, or otherwiſe;
' To continue, and make Peace, or War,
' with any Prince or People, that are not
' Chriſtians, in any Places of our Trade,
' as ſhall be moſt for our Advantage and
' Benefit. And alſo to Right and Recom-
' pence our ſelves upon the Goods, Eſtate,
' or People of thoſe Parts, by whom we
' ſhall ſuſtain any Injury, Loſs, or Da-
' mage; or upon any other People what-
' ſoever, that ſhall any way interrupt,
' wrong, or injure us in our ſaid Trade.
' And that we may ſeize the Perſons of
' ſuch *Engliſh*, or others of His Majeſty's
' Subjects, in the ſaid *Eaſt-Indies*, which
' ſhall Sail in any *Indian*, or *Engliſh* Veſ-
' ſel, or inhabit in thoſe Parts without
' our Licence, and ſend them to *Eng-*
' *land.*

' Now We the ſaid Governor and Com-
' pany having an undoubted Right by
' ancient Stipulation with the King of
' *Perſia*, that we ſhall have for ever Half
' the Cuſtoms of his Port of *Gombroone;*
' and that our Agent ſhall have Seſſion in
' his *Divan*, or Council; and that an Of-
' ficer

'ficer of ours fhall always be permitted
'to Sit in his *Bundar*, or Cuftom-Houfe,
'to Colleĉt Half the Cuftoms of his faid
'Port of *Gombroone*. Which Privilege
'was ftipulated, and granted to our Com-
'pany formerly, in Confideration of the
'*Englifh* Blood and Treafure, fpent in Af-
'fifting his Predeceffors, Kings of *Perfia*,
'in Taking the Ifland *Ormus* from the
'*Portugueze*, which in thofe Times de-
'priv'd his Empire of all Trade.

'And whereas the faid King of *Perfia*,
'or his Minifters, have for many Years
'laft paft depriv'd us of our Ancient Pri-
'vileges before recited, and have put off
'our Agents with the Payment only of
'One Thoufand Tomands yearly, inftead
'of 40000 Tomands, which our Moiety
'of the Cuftoms of *Gombroone* amounts
'unto: Upon which a Debt of above
'One Hundred Fifty Thoufand Tomands
'has accru'd to us; which we have often
'without Effeĉt demanded of Him, the
'faid King, and his Minifters:

'We do therefore here, by Virtue of
'the Authority granted unto Us by His
'Majefty, our Sovereign Lord the King,
E   'as

' as aforefaid, empower and authorize you
' to invade, and make War upon the faid
' King of *Perfia*, and his Subjects, by Sea,
' and by Land, as you fhall fee Caufe;
' and to feize and take any of the Ships,
' or Goods, properly belonging to the faid
' King of *Perfia*, or any of his Subjects;
' and that you deliver the fame to our
' Governor and Council at *Bombay*, for
' our Ufe; together with all the Invoices,
' Books, and Bills of Loading, and Pa-
' pers, you fhall find on Board any Ship
' belonging to the faid King of *Perfia*, or
' any of his Subjects.

' But you are in no wife to offer any
' Violence to any of the Goods, Perfons,
' or Eftates of any of the King of *Indo-*
' *ftan*'s Subjects, or any other Prince or
' State in *India*, in Amity with His Ma-
' jefty and Us. And if you fhall find
' Goods belonging to the Subjects of the
' King of *Perfia*, on Board any *India* Ship,
' or Junk, belonging to any King, or
' Prince in Amity with His Majefty, and
' this Company, as aforefaid; you fhall
' only take out thofe Numerical Goods,
' which do belong to the Subjects of the
' King of *Perfia*: And fhall alfo duly pay
' unto

' unto the Captain, or Commander of
' fuch *Indian* Ship, or Veſſel in Amity,
' as aforeſaid, the juſt Freight condition'd
' to be paid, if thoſe Goods had been du-
' ly landed in *Perſia*, according to Bills of
' Loading.

   ' But becauſe the End of all War is
' Peace, we would have you (after you
' have taken near what you think may
' make us Satisfction) to give Notice to
' the King of *Perſia*'s Governor at *Gom-*
' *broone*, That if he will pay you down
' Fifty Thouſand Tomands preſently, you
' have Power to diſcharge the King of
' *Perſia* of all Arrears of Cuſtoms due to
' the Company. And that you will deli-
' ver all that you have taken, truly and
' faithfully, to the Reſpective Owners, or
' to the Governor for their Uſe; the Go-
' vernor engaging to you, that for the fu-
' ture He, and his Succeſſors, ſhall duly
' pay the Company Ten Thouſand To-
' mands yearly, in full of their growing
. Cuſtom of *Gombroone*.

   ' And you may promiſe on our Parts,
' that we will ſend yearly a Ship of ſuch
' Force as yours, or Two of Half the

        ' Force,

' Force, to Guard and Defend the *Perſian*
' Ports, againſt the Infolences and Af-
' fronts of the *Portugueze*. And what-
' foever you ſhall receive on this Account
' in Money, you are to pay unto our Pre-
' fident and Council at *Surat*, for the Com-
' pany's Uſe.

' Tho' We have begun theſe Inſtructi-
' ons to you, with and concerning your
' *Perſia* Voyage, which was firſt in our
' Intention; yet our Affairs having much
' alter'd ſince that Intent, You are in the
' firſt place, and with the firſt fair Wind,
' after your Arrival in the *Downs*, to Sail
' to our Iſland St. *Helena;* and there to
' deliver to our Governor and Council, all
' Soldiers, and other Things ſhipp'd on
' Board you for that Place: And during
' your Stay there, you are to be Second
' of our Council upon that Iſland; and,
' ſo far as in you lies, to further the Exe-
' cution and Performance of all ſuch Or-
' ders, as we have given our ſaid Gover-
' nor and Council, for the better Govern-
' ment and Regulation of our People and
' Intereſt there.

' Being

' Being difpatch'd from thence in as
' fhort a Time as poffibly you can; you
' are immediately to Sail for *Pepper-Bay*,
' within the Streights of *Sanda*, near *Ban-*
' *tam*; firft Standing into a Small Bay at
' the *South* Side of the *Weft* End of *Ja-*
' *va*. In one of which Places, you will
' meet with fome of our Ships, or Intelli-
' gences from them, now bound out for
' *Bantam*, under the Command of Sir
' *John Wetwang*, or of Captain *John Ni-*
' *cholfon*; You agreeing in Writing, be-
' fore you go, by what Signs you may
' know any of our Ships at a Diftance,
' belonging to either of thofe Fleets.

' As foon as you meet with each of our
' faid Fleets, if Sir *John Wetwang* be
' prefent, you are to Command as Vice-
' Admiral; if He be abfent, as Admiral
' of our faid Fleet; and to follow fuch
' Orders, jointly or feverally, as we have
' given to our Agent *Englifh*, or Coun-
' cil, or fhall hereafter give to our Admi-
' ral, Sir *John Wetwang*, and his Coun-
' cil of War.

' After

'After your Difpatch from *Bantam*,
'you are to proceed upon your firft in-
'tended *Perfia* Voyage, with one of our
'Sloops in your Company; if it fhall be
'fo thought convenient at a Council of
'War.

'And in the whole Progrefs of your
'Voyage, at all Places, you are to put
'thofe Powers intrufted to Us by His
'Majefty's Charter, recited before in this
'Commiffion, into effectual Execution,
'with your beft Skill and Difcretion, a-
'gainft Interlopers, and all others, that
'fhall violate His Majefty's Juft Autho-
'rity.

'And whatfoever you fhall feize or take
'by Virtue of this, or any other Com-
'miffion deriv'd from His Majefty, at St.
'*Helena*, you are to deliver to our Gover-
'nor and Council there; and in other
'Places, to our Governor and Council at
'*Bombay;* taking at each Place their re-
'fpective Receipts, for the Particulars of
'what you deliver them; for the Ufe,
'One Half of His Majefty, the other Half
'for our felves. Except only what you
'fhall

' fhall take from the King of *Perfia*, or his
' Subjects, which only and properly be-
' long to the Company.

' God fending you to *Bombay* or *Surat*,
' after your *Perfia* Voyage, you are to
' leave all our Soldiers at *Bombay*, for a
' Supply to our Garifon there; and to fol-
' low at *Surat* all fuch further Orders, as
' you fhall receive from our Prefident and
' Council, for your Loading and Voyage
' Home to *England*, according to your
' Charter-Party. Given under our Com-
' mon Seal, the Seven and twentieth Day
' of *July, Anno Dom.* 1683.

Seal'd with the Company's
Seal, in the Prefence
of

E. Portmans.
Richard Harris.

Thefe

Thefe feveral Orders, by the Affiftance
of God, he executed, to the great Satif-
faction of the *Eaft-India* Company; and
purfu'd their Inftructions relating to *Perfia*
to that Advantage, that he procur'd Satif-
faction for all the Injuries done the Company from the King of *Perfia*; and receiv'd at Two feveral Payments from the
Agent of that Prince, about Four Hundred Thoufand Tomands, for the Company's Ufe.   He renew'd alfo the Ancient
Privileges granted to the Company, with
other extraordinary Liberties of Traffick.

Befides this, he took Poffeffion of *Hip-
pons*, alias *Princes-Ifle*, in the Name of
His Majefty, for the Service of the Company.   And when he had taken it, he
gave it the Name of *Carolus Secundus*
Ifle, and fix'd the King's Standard there.
It was inhabited by a People, that depend-
ed upon thofe of *Java*.

When he had finifh'd the Affairs where-
in he was engag'd in thofe Parts, he Sail'd
to *Mufcat* in *Arabia Felix*; where alfo
he narrowly efcap'd with his Life, upon
                                                        this

this Occafion. In the Evening, coming from that City, and taking his Barge to go on Board his Ship; a Centinel, from the Shore, fir'd a Shot, which pafs'd betwixt him and his Coxon. Upon this, he wav'd his Sword in a threatning manner at him. Of which he was altogether regardlefs, and fir'd again; but the Bullet graz'd upon the Water, and was fpent before it reach'd the Boat. The next Morning, he was fully refolv'd upon Receiving fome Satisfaction for the Affront; tho' it was pretended, that the Cuftom of the Place allow'd no Boat to go off, after fuch a Time in the Evening. However, this was not fatisfactory to his Refentment; and therefore, he order'd his Surgeon to carry the following Letter to the Governor.

S I R,

'GO on Shore, and pray Mr. *Stephens* to go with you to the Governor, 'to interpret to him what is here under- 'written.

F   'Let

'Let him know, that I fent you to de-
' mand Satisfaction, for the Great Affront
' which was given yefterday in the Even-
' ing, to the King my Mafter, before it
' was dark :

    ' Firft, By being fir'd at, when the
' King of *England*'s Flag was flying in
' the Boat; which is a Breach of the
' Peace.

    ' Next, For wounding One of my
' Men in his Arm; which may endan-
' ger his Life; and for being in Dan-
' ger of my Life my felf.

    ' And all this was done, without Cal-
' ling, or making a Noife; a Thing unu-
' fual in any Garrifon or Fort in the
' World, and contrary to the Law of
' Arms; and can aim at nothing but pri-
' vate Murther.

    ' I therefore declare, I will never fet
' my Foot on Shore in Peace, without
' they fend me on Board the pretended
' Centinel, to punifh according to his De-
                       ' fert.

' fert. Or that the Governor will be
' pleas'd to order him publick Punifhment,
' at the Place where the Boat came on
' Shore, and in the Sight of all *Englifh-*
' *men* here.

' If he refuses, let him know from me,
' that if I meet their whole Fleet at Sea,
' or Part of them, I fhall give Satisfaction
' to my felf by them.

' The *Dutch* told me, when they were
' here, they went and came all Hours of
' the Night, as they pleas'd.

' Let him know, I am an *Englifhman;*
' and value my felf in this One Ship, as
' much as if 20 Sail of *Dutch* were here;
' and expect to receive as much Privilege
' and Kindnefs. But if they fhow their
' Kindnefs to the *Dutch* for Fear; I expect
' they fhould do the fame to the *Englifh*
' for Love.

' This is not the Firft, Second, or Third
' time they have abus'd the *Englifh*, who
' always give Refpect to Strangers. I am
' a Friend, or otherwife, as they pleafe,

THO. GRANTHAM.

F 2 This

This Meſſage put the Governor into ſuch Confuſion, that he immediately ſummon'd his Council, to adviſe what Method was moſt proper for putting a Period to this Diſturbance. They resolv'd therefore to come on Board him, and to heal the Diſguſt that he had taken, by a very ſignificant *Piſcaſh*, or Preſent. But beſides this, he inſiſted upon the Liberty to be granted to all the *Engliſh*, of Paſſing to and fro in their Boats, at what time they pleas'd. And this they ſubmitted to likewiſe under their Hands and Seals: Which Indulgence he deliver'd aftewards to the *Engliſh* General.

For they knew very well, that his Ship was of that Force, that ſhe was able both to annoy their Fort, and burn their Veſſels in the Harbour; and this render'd them ſo very tractable and obſequious to his Demands.

When he arriv'd at *Bombay*, which was on the Third of *November*, 1684. he was inform'd, that one *Richard Keigwin* had, the Year before his Arrival, uſurp'd the Government, impriſon'd the Governor, Mr. *Charles Ward*, and broke in upon the Charter

Charter of the *East-India* Company; granting Liberty of Trade to all the Parts of *India, Arabia,* and *Persia;* and granted Passes to the Ships Trading in those Parts; a Copy of one of which is this: *V I Z.*

V I V A T   R E X.

To all Kings, Princes and Gover-
nors of Countries, Commanders
of Ships, or Others, the well-
affected Friends of the most Po-
tent King of Great - Britain,
France *and* Ireland, *Defender*
of the Faith, &c.

‘ *C*HARLES the *Second,* by the Grace
‘ of God, of *England,* &c. doth,
‘ by His Honourable Governor, *Richard*
‘ *Keigwin,* Esq; grant and give Free Li-
‘ berty of Trade, to all his Subjects be-
‘ longing to the Port and Island of *Bom-*
‘ *bay;* and to Navigate their Ships to all
‘ Ports and Parts of *India, Persia,* and *A-*
‘ *rabia,* &c.

‘ There-

' Therefore, Captain *Henry Gary*, Mer-
' chant, and Freeholder of *Bombay*, Own-
' er of the Good Ship *Ruparrel*, whereof
' goes *Pedro Domell* Commander; has this
' Pafs in His Majefty's Name, from his
' faid Honourable Governor.

' That all Kings, Princes, and Gover-
' nors of Dominions, Countries and Pro-
' vinces, and Ports, give the faid Ship,
' Commanders and Merchants, free and
' friendly Permiffion, to have free Ingrefs
' and Egrefs, in and out of their Domini-
' ons, Countries and Ports, as they are
' His Majefty of *Great-Britain*'s Subjects;
' receiving them kindly and courteoufly,
' upon Payment of the Lawful and Ufual
' Cuftoms, and other Duties of the Ports,
' this Ship may touch at; and granting
' the said Commanders and Merchants
' thereof, to have all Right of Navigati-
' on, Traffick and Commerce. Which
' Courteous Civilities will be moft accepta-
' ble to His moft Serene Majefty of *Great-*
' *Britain*, and always thankfully acknow-
' ledg'd by his Subjects.

' That

'That all Ships, Veffels or Boats, be-
' longing to any Kings or Princes, His Ma-
' jefty's Royal Friends, this Ship fhall at
' any Time or Place meet with, fuffer her
' to pafs without Seizure, Moleftation, or
' Trouble, not offering any Abufe or Inci-
' vility to the said Ship, Goods, or Per-
' fons on Board; but aid and affift her in
' all Cafes of Want, Hazard, or Danger.
' Which Friendly Ufage from Comman-
' ders of such Ships, Veffels or Boats, will
' demonftrate their well-affected Amity to
' His Majefty of *Great-Britain*, and en-
' gage his Subjects to a perpetual Conferva-
' tion of the same with them.

' Thefe are requefted and defir'd from
' all Kings, Princes and Governors, and
' Commanders of Ships, during the Term
' of this Pafs, which is for One whole
' Year, commencing from *January* the 1ft,
' One Thousand Six Hundred Eighty and
' Three. Given under my Hand and Seal,
' with His Majefty's Union-Seal, at His
' Majefty's Fort of *Bombay*, *Jan.* 1. 168$\frac{3}{4}$.

RICHARD KEIGWIN.

J. Thorburn, Secretary.

Thus

Thus, under the Specious Pretence of Loyalty, the pretended Governor, and his Adherents, skreen'd the moſt Execrable Villany, diſguiz'd their deteſtable Rebellion, under the Name of Duty and Obedience, and traiterouſly made uſe of His Majeſty's Authority, to patronize their Revolt and Uſurpation.

And therefore, he fairly repreſented to them, not only the Heinous Proceedings they had engag'd in, and the deſperate Folly they had committed, but the direful and fatal Conſequences that would attend all ſuch unlawful and deſtructive Attempts. This Repreſentation ſtartl'd them into a Pannick Diſtruſt of their unhappy Condition, and put them into ſuch an amazing Fear, as made them dread the ſame Fate that ſeveral of them had undergone.

For the Governor, Mr. *Ward*, was inclin'd to proſecute them with Severity, only he interpos'd with him by Mildneſs and gentle Perſwaſions, rather to propoſe a Pardon to them, upon their Laying down their Arms, and returning to their Obedience.

He

He alfo engag'd his Intereft and Application, for Procuring them a Pardon from
the King, and the Company.

Upon this, they drew up feveral Articles relating to their full and abfolute Pardon, and a Freedom from all Law-Suits
and Moleftations, upon the Account of
their preceding Mutiny and Difturbance.

Thefe Articles he willingly fign'd, and
afterwards took Poffeffion of the Fort and
Caftle of *Bombay, November* the 20th.
1684. And then mufter'd all the Officers
and Soldiers in his own Name.

For he was empower'd by the Presfi-
dent and Council of *Surat*, to treat with
the Mutineers, and make what Amicable
Agreement and Conclufion with them he
was able.

He was forc'd to continue the Government upon himfelf for Ten Weeks, till
Mr. *Charles Zinzan* arriv'd from *Surat*,
from whence he was fent by the General to
fucceed him.

The Occafion of this Rebellion, which
he has given an Account of, was this.
Mr. *Boucher*, who had been employ'd by
the Company, was turn'd out of their
Service; and living at *Surat*, made his
G Houfe

Houſe a Receptacle for the Interlopers, who found him very ſerviceable to their Occaſions and Neceſſities.

At the ſame time alſo, one Mr. *Petit* was turn'd out of his Employment under the Company; and being both of them therefore diſaffected to the Company's Affairs, encourag'd this Diſobedience in *Keigwin* and his Followers, and animated their Defection.

This *Petit* bought a Ship at *Bombay*, and fitted her out, under the Protection of the Rebels. But as he was Sailing to viſit *Boucher* at *Surat*, the *Sanganians* met with him near the High Land of St. *John*'s, and wounded him ſo dangerouſly, that he afterwards dy'd, and his Ship was blown up, and all her Lading deſtroy'd.

The Day before this Action happen'd, Sir *Thomas* was Sailing from *Surat*, in order to reduce *Bombay*. Which as ſoon as, by the good Providence of God, he did, and had taken Poſſeſſion of it, he found mounted on the Fort 114 Pieces of Cannon, and in it 600 Barrels of Powder, with all other Things neceſſary for a long Defence, and 500 Officers and Soldiers in Pay.

Keig-

Keigwin, who was more fenfible of his Danger than the reft, he prevail'd upon fooner to furrender himfelf, and alfo to deliver him 12 Bags of Gold, which they had taken out of the Ship *Return,* and which he put on Board his own.

While *Keigwin* and He were making Propofals to the reft, they hifs'd at them, and with loud Exclamations, cry'd, *No Governor, but* Keigwin; *and if he will not hold, we will confirm another.* And had not the Good Providence of God prevented his Deftruction, he had fallen very cowardly murther'd by the Hands of one *Harwood,* a Soldier. For this Fellow, in the Crowd, prefented a Piftol loaden with a Brace of Bullets to his Back; which Captain *Henry Fletcher* feeing, he took hold of it, and diverted the malicious, fatal Stroke.

To fecure to Captain *Keigwin,* and the reft of the Seditious, an Exemption from the Punifhment they juftly deferv'd, Sir *Thomas* willingly yielded, and furrender'd himfelf Hoftage to them, till fuch Time as Sir *John Child,* who was then at *Surat,* and General of *India,* fhould fign, ratify, and confirm the Pardon which was propos'd to them. Which accordingly was

G 2   done

done in a little time afterwards, to the great Satisfaction of the Criminals.

About this Time, there was an *English* Ship feiz'd and taken by the *Portugueze*, and carried into *Baſſene*, an Iſland not far diſtant from *Bombay*. Which, as foon as he heard of, he fent this following Letter to the Captain-General of the *Portugueze* for the *North*.

Bombay-Fort, *Nov.* 24.
1684.

SIR,

I Underſtand by a Letter receiv'd from Baſſene, *that you, or ſome of your Ships, have ſeiz'd and taken a Ship belonging to my Maſter the King of* England's *Subjects, living at* Maderas. *Which Ship I left at* Muſcat, *with Directions to Sail after me to* Bombay, *or* Surat. *I much wonder how you dare do ſuch ill Things, and likewiſe give ſo great an Affront to His moſt Sacred Majeſty, my King.* Sir, *If you do not forthwith, upon Sight hereof, clear and diſcharge the ſaid Ship, making full Satisfaction for all Damages the Own-*

ers

ers and Commanders have suftain'd by you; Know, that I will come, and fetch Her out of your Harbour, and perhaps ſhake Hands with you at Salſet, *which of Right belongs to my Maſter, who is King of theſe Seas, and whoſe Right I am in Duty bound to maintain in theſe Parts. So expecting a ready and friendly Compliance, or elſe you muſt take what will follow; becauſe I know very well your Readineſs to abuſe and murder* Englishmen. *This from your Friend, if I find Cauſe, and whom you may oblige,*

THO. GRANTHAM.

Theſe Threats had ſo good an Effect upon the General, that they aw'd him into Juſtice and Civility, and forc'd him to quit his ill-gotten Prize.

Having thus manag'd the great Truſt repos'd in him by the Honourable *Eaſt-India* Company, with that Fidelity and Care that became his Charge and Station, he took his Leave of *India*, and Sail'd back again for *England*.

Where,

Where, in a little time after his Return, his moſt Gracious Sovereign, the Late King *James* II. preſented him with a Valuable Gold Chain and Medal, in Conſideration of thoſe Momentous Affairs, that he had manag'd abroad with ſuch remarkable Succeſs.   And alſo he receiv'd, upon the ſame Account, a Noble Gratuity from the Honourable *Eaſt-India* Company.

For Great Minds are never unmindful of Great Services; but the more you endeavour to oblige them, the more you provoke them to out-do, even the moſt Meritorious Performances, by a Liberal Compenſation.

After the Departure of King *James* for *France*, and the Peaceable Settlement of King *William* and His Royal Conſort in *England*, he was ſworn One of His Majeſty's moſt Honourable Privy-Chamber; and was appointed by the Earl of *Dorſet*, then Lord Chamberlain, to attend in that Quality at the Coronation; and receiv'd this Order for that Purpoſe.

April

April the 6th.
1689.

S I R,

*H**IS Majesty having appointed You
to be One of His most Honourable
Privy-Chamber in Ordinary, You are, by
the Duty of your Place, particularly oblig'd
to attend on His Royal Person, at his Coronation; which is to be on the Eleventh Day
of* April *instant, at* Westminster. *You are
therefore hereby requir'd to give your At-
tendance at that time, to go in the Proceedings, according to your Place and Quality.
Thus I rest,*

Your Affectionate Friend
to Serve You,

D O R S E T.

To *Sir* Thomas Grantham.

Towards

Towards the Conclusion of this same
Year, he was also admitted and sworn into
the Station of Esquire of the Body to His
Majesty K. *William*, according to the Tenor
of these Words:

‘ THese are to Certify whom it may
‘   concern, That by Virtue of a
‘ Warrant to me directed, from the Right
‘ Honourable *CHARLES* Earl of *Dor-*
‘*set* and *Middlesex*, Lord Chamberlain
‘ of His Majesty’s Houshold; I have sworn
‘ and admitted Sir *Thomas Grantham*, Kt.
‘ into the Place and Quality of Esquire
‘ of the Body to His Majesty’s Royal Per-
‘ son in Ordinary; to have and enjoy all
‘ Fees, Rights, Dues, Salaries, Profits,
‘ Perquisites, and all other Advantages
‘ whatsoever to that Place belonging, or
‘ any ways appertaining. In witness where-
‘ of I have hereunto set my Hand and Seal,
‘ this present 18th of *September*, *A. D.*
‘ 1689. in the First Year of Their Maje-
‘ sties Reign. ✻

Fleetwood Shepherd.

Thefe

Thefe were the Dignities he was in-
vefted with under the Government of
King *William* and Queen *Mary*, of Glorious and Immortal Memory.

And when Her Prefent Majefty afcend-
ed the Throne of Her Celebrated Ance-
ftor's, to which Her Royal Virtues, had
the Kingdom been Elective, like *Poland*,
would have entitl'd Her, without De-
fcent, by a General Approbation; he was
admitted by the Right Honourable the
Earl of *Jerfey*, then Lord Chamberlain,
into the Place and Quality of One of the
Gentlemen of Her Majefty's moft Honourable Privy-Chamber, the 17th of *April*,
in the Firft Year of Her Reign. Which,
if it ftill goes on with thofe progreflive
Marks of Glory and Renown, with
which Providence has fignaliz'd its Beginning, it will be as much the Admiration
of future Ages, as it is the Joy and Tri-
umph of the prefent. And were it not
that her Government has been ruffl'd with
the Difturbance of a Foreign War, and
thofe mifchievous Confequences that attend it, the Reign of Queen *ANNE* would
be in other Terms the Golden Age, and

H　　　　　　　　　　　Peace

Peace would have vy'd with Plenty. But notwithſtanding the Neighb'ring Diſturber of our Peace, She has been highly inſtrumental in producing a very uſeful and pleaſant Harmony out of Diſcord, of Confederating different Perſwaſions Abroad, and Uniting, as much as poſſible, diſſonant Parties at Home, into a League of perfect Amity and Friendſhip.

And that the Families of ſuch who have merited well of their King and Country, might receive ſome Credit and Satiſfaction, from the Brave and Publick Performances of their Predeceſſors, and ſhare in the Reputation of them; he has had the Privilege of an Addition made to his Paternal Coat of Arms, upon the Account of thoſe Serviceable and Adventurous Actions that are mention'd in this Hiſtory: Which I ſhall conclude with the Draught of a Warrant, from the Right Honourable the Lord Marſhal, to *Garter* and *Clarenceux*, Kings of Arms, for making Additions to the Arms, and Alteration in the Creſt, of Sir *Thomas Grantham*, Knight.

' Where-

'WHereas Sir *Thomas Grantham*, of
' Batavia-Houfe, within the Pa-
' rifh of *Sonbury*, in the County of *Mid-*
' *dlefex*, Knight, One of the Gentlemen
' in Ordinary of Her Majefty's moft Ho-
' nourable Privy-Chamber, and Efquire for
' the Queen's Body at Her Royal Coronati-
' on; in both which Stations he likewife
' ferv'd the late King *William* and Queen
' *Mary*, of Glorious and Immortal Me-
' mory; having alfo been One of the
' Directors of *Greenwich* Hofpital, from
' its Firft Foundation; has humbly repre-
' fented unto me, That He, and his Fa-
' ther, Mr. *Thomas Grantham*, of *Biffiter*,
' alias *Burnceffer*, *in Com. Oxon.* (who
' loft his Life at the Siege of *Oxford*, *An.*
' 1645, in the Caufe of the Royal Mar-
' tyr) have commonly us'd thefe Arms;
' viz. *Ermin a Griphon Rampant*, *Gules*,
' *beak'd and member'd*, *azure*; and for
' their Creft, on a *Wreath*, a *Moor*'s, or
' *Saracen*'s *Head*, *Coup'd Proper;* which
' were, as he conceives, the Arms born
' by his Grandfather, Mr. *Richard Grant-*
' *ham*, a Defcendant of the Ancient Fa-

H 2 ' mily

' mily of *Grantham* in *Lincolnſhire*: Pray-
' ing me to iſſue my Warrant to ſome of
' the Kings of Arms, for making ſuch Ad-
' ditions to the ſaid Coat, and Alteration
' in the Creſt, as may moſt properly de-
' note, and preſerve in Memory, ſome Ne-
' table Exploits he has perform'd for his
' Prince and Country, as well as diſtin-
' guiſh him and his Poſterity, from all
' others of that Name or Family.

   ' And foraſmuch as the ſaid Sir *Thomas*
' *Grantham*, being Maſter of the Ship *Ed-*
' *ward* and *Jane* of *London*, was, by
' Commiſſion from Sir *William Berkley*, Kt.
' Governor and Captain-General of *Vir-*
' *ginia*, dated the Second of *April*, 1673.
' as One of the Ableſt Commanders, con-
' ſtituted and appointed Admiral of a Fleet
' of Merchant-Men, conſiſting of 25 Sail,
' from thence; which, in thoſe Times of
' Danger, occaſion'd by the War with the
' *States-General* of the United Provinces,
' he convey'd ſafe Home.

   ' And making another Voyage thither
' in the Ship *Concord*, a Veſſel of 500
' Tons, carrying 32 Guns, and between
                     ' Forty

' Forty and Fifty Men; upon his Arrival
' there, *Anno* 1676, finding the Country
' in open Rebellion, fomented by Mr. *Na-*
' *thaniel Bacon*, and other turbulent Spi-
' rits, who had taken Arms, and not only
' forc'd the Governor, Sir *William Berk-*
' *ly* aforemention'd, with moſt of the
' Council and Chief Inhabitants, to fly to
' a Place call'd *Accomack*, on the *North*
' Side of *Cape-Henry;* but, in Contempt
' of His Majeſty's Authority, burnt the
' Houſe where the Publick Aſſembly and
' Courts of Juſtice are held, at *James-*
' *City*: He, the ſaid Sir *Thomas Grant-*
' *ham*, in Purſuance of his Duty, ap-
' prov'd himſelf to be a Man worthy of
' ſingular Eſteem, for his very prudent
' Conduct; having, by means of a per-
' ſonal Acquaintance, formerly between
' him and ſome of the principal Officers
' among the Rebels; at the utmoſt Hazard
' of his Life, with exceeding great Ho-
' nour and Fidelity, ſo ſucceſsfully tranſ-
' acted Matters, as partly by Perſwaſion,
' and partly by Compulſion and Strata-
' gem, to reduce that Colony to their juſt
' Allegiance, and entirely Reſettle the Go-
' vernment on its former Baſis. For which
' extra-

'extraordinary Service, his Sacred Maje-
'fty King *Charles* the Second moft graci-
'oufly beftow'd upon him, at his Return
'to *England*, a Noble Donative.

   'In which faid Ship, the *Concord*, Sail-
'ing again for *Virginia*, he was, the 25th
'of *October*, 1678, about 120 Leagues
'from the Land's-End, attack'd by *Cana-*
'*ry* a *Spanifh* Renegado, and Admiral of
'the King of *Algiers*, in a new Frigot
'of 48 Guns, call'd the *Rofe*, carrying
'upwards of 600 Men; and defended
'himfelf with fuch undaunted Courage
'and Bravery, that altho' he had only 22
'Guns, and 50 Men, including the Paf-
'fengers, after Two or Three Hours fharp
'Difpute, having been Thrice boarded
'by the *Barbarians;* who, enrag'd be-
'caufe they could not get the Maftery,
'fir'd him on the Quarter, and the
'Mizon-Yard being fhot down, fir'd the
'Sail; which burnt very vehemently,
'and immediately fet all the latter Part
'of the Ship on Fire; yet he ftill con-
'tinued his Fight, keeping the Round-
'Houfe and Cuddy, till oblig'd by the
'Heat to retire, (all that Accompanied
                      'him,

' him, being either Kill'd or Wounded,)
' and then getting down into his great
' Cabin and Steerage, Sallied out with thofe
' that were there; refolving rather to pe-
' rifh in the Flames, than yield: But in
' the *Interim*, the *Turk*'s Fore-Sail hanging
' in the Brails over the *Concord*'s Poop, and
' taking Fire, he would fain have got off;
' which the faid Sir *Thomas Grantham* en-
' deavouring to prevent, by fetching down
' with fmall Shot, as many as run up to
' cut him clear, until his Sails, Mafts,
' Shrouds and Yards, were all in a Blaze,
' when cutting the Enemy loofe, prefently
' their Maft to the Deck went by the
' Board, with many Men in its Top, and
' his bloody Flag; feveral of the Crew
' betaking themfelves to their Boats. How-
' ever, at laft, both Sides overcoming the
' Fire, and there being little or no Wind,
' Admiral *Canary*, with the Help of his
' Oars, Row'd, till he was out of Shot,
' otherwife poffibly, many Chriftian Slaves
' might have been Releas'd. But having
' loft abundance of his Men, and the next
' Morning it proving a fmall Gale, he ftood
' away, and left Sir *Thomas* to purfue his
' Courfe; whofe fignal Behaviour in this
' defpe-

2

' defperate Engagement, juftly gain'd him
' the higheft Reputation and Applaufe:
' Infomuch, that his faid Majefty, out of
' a Princely Regard to fuch tranfcendent
' Valour, gave him a Gold Chain and
' Medal of great Value. And afterwards,
' as a diftinguifhing Teftimony of his ha-
' ving given fuch Proofs of his Abilities,
' Courage and Loyalty, upon thefe feveral
' Occafions, which deferv'd to receive all
' fitting Encouragement, was pleas'd, as
' a Mark of his Royal Favour to him, by
' fpecial Mandat, under the Signet and
' Sign Manual, 3d of *March*, 168$\frac{1}{2}$. to
' recommend him in a moft particular
' Manner, to the Governor and Company
' of *Merchants* Trading to the *Eaft-Indies*;
' that he, and the Ship which he intended
' to Build, might be Entertain'd by them.
' Which Ship, being Built accordingly,
' Burthen 816 Tuns, carrying 64 Guns,
' and 300 Men, the faid King, and his
' Royal Highnefs the Duke of *York*, Lord
' High Admiral, *&c.* attended by divers of
' the Nobility, did him the Honour to be
' prefent at the Lanching thereof, when
' His Majefty nam'd Her, *Charles the Se-*
' *cond.* And as a farther Acknowledgment
of

' of the faid Sir *Thomas Grantham*'s Emi-
' nent Deferts, Knighted him on Board
' the faid Ship at *Deptford*, the 18th of
' *February*, *Anno* 168². After which, he
' obtain'd the *Eaft-India* Company's Com-
' miffion, dated the 27th of *July*, 1683;
' empowering and authorizing him to in-
' vade, and make War upon the King of
' *Perfia*, and his Subjects, by Sea and
' Land; and to feize, and take any of the
' Ships and Goods, properly belonging to
' the faid King of *Perfia*, or any of his
' Subjects, in Reprizal for a Debt of 150
' Thoufand Tomands, accruing to the
' Company, for a Moiety of the Cu-
' ftoms of *Gombroone*, often without effect
' demanded; and which, among other An-
' cient Privileges, they had been depriv'd
' of by the faid King of *Perfia*'s Mini-
' fters: tho' it was ftipulated, and grant-
' ed to them formerly, in Confideration of
' the *Englifh* Blood and Treafure, fpent in
' Affifting his Predeceffors, Kings of *Per-*
' *fia*, in Taking the Ifland *Ormus* from the
' *Portugueze*, which in thofe Times de-
' priv'd the Empire of all Trade. But,
' with Inftructions, in the firft place, to
' Sail to St. *Helena*, and during his Stay

I ' there,

'there, to be Second of the Company's
'Council upon that Iiland. From whence
'he was to iteer to *Pepper-Bay*, within the
'Streights of *Sanda*, near *Bantam;* firit
'Standing into a imall Bay, at the *South*
'Side of the *West* End of *Java*.

'In one of which Places, in meeting
'with iome of the Company's Ships, then
'bound out for *Bantam*, under the Com-
'mand of Sir *John Wetwang*, or of Cap-
'tain *John Nicholson;* if Sir *John Wet-
'wang* was preient, He, the iaid Sir *Tho-
'mas Grantham* was to Command as Vice-
'Admiral; but if abient, as Admiral of
'the iaid Fleet; and thence to proceed
'upon the *Persia* Voyage, with one of
'their Sloops in his Company, if it ihould
'be io thought convenient at a Council of
'War, *&c.*

'All which Powers and Directions he
'io happily executed, as to acquire from
'the King of *Persia*'s Agents, for the Com-
'pany, about 400 Thouiand Pounds in
'Money, at Two Payments, and full Re-
'ititution of their Ancient Rights, with
'other Advantages of Commerce.

'And

'And moreover, took Poffeffion in the 'King's Name, on their Behalf, of *Hip-* '*pons*, alias *Princes-Ifle*, inhabited by a 'People dependant on *Java*; giving it 'the Name of *Carolus Secundus* Ifle.

'Nor was he lefs Succefsful in Serving 'the Company, on his Arriving at *Bom-* '*bay*. For, Coming to an Anchor in the 'Bay, *November* the 3d, 1684, and recei- 'ving Intelligence, that a Revolution 'had been made the 27th of *December*, 'the Year preceding, by one *Richard* '*Keigwin*, and his Abettors; who, ufurp- 'ing the Government, imprifon'd Mr. '*Charles Ward*, their Governor, there; 'and granted free Liberty of Trade to 'all His Majefty's Subjects belonging to 'that Port and Ifland, and to Navigate 'their Ships to all Parts and Ports of *In-* '*dia*, *Perfia*, and *Arabia*, &c. with all 'Right of Navigation, Traffick, and Com- 'merce; contrary to the Royal Charter of 'the King's moft Excellent Majefty, bear- 'ing Date the 3d of *April* 1661, & 13. '*Regni fui*, appropriating to the Company 'the entire Trade of the *Eaft-Indies*, and

I 2   'decla-

' declaring, that the Ports, Cities, Towns
' and Places thereof, fhould not be traded
' unto, vifited, frequented, or haunt-
' ed by any of His Majefty's Subjects,
' without their Licence, &c. He, the
' faid Sir *Thomas Grantham*, lay by, till
' he fecur'd, and cut off Twenty two of
' their Ships and Veffels, laded with Pro-
' vifions and Merchandize; and then
' Landing the 20th of *November*, with
' 250 Men, in the Night, furpriz'd the
' Caftle and Fort, which had 114 Pieces
' of Cannon mounted, making himfelf
' Mafter thereof. Whereupon he reliev'd
' the aforefaid Mr. *Ward* from his Confine-
' ment, retriev'd to the Value of 12 Thou-
' fand Pounds of the Company's Treafure,
' that had been treacheroufly feiz'd in the
' Ship *Return*, and without Effufion of
' Blood, reclaim'd both Soldiers and Inha-
' bitants to their due Obedience, by the
' feafonable Offer of Indemnity, and a
' general Pardon; which he afterwards
' procur'd to be ratified, confirm'd, and
' fign'd on Board the *Charles the Second*,
' at the River's Mouth of *Surat* the 2d of
' *February*, 168$\frac{4}{5}$, by the Honourable
' *John Child*, fince created Baronet, Pre-
' fident of *India*, &c.

' And

'And the faid Sir *Thomas Grantham*
'having, while he ftay'd in the faid Port of
'*Bombay*, exercis'd the Office of Gover-
'nor of the Caftle, Fort, and Ifland, with
'much Prudence and Integrity, render'd
'it up to the Perfon, whom the aforefaid
'Prefident, and Council of the *Indies* did
'nominate to that Command.

'And upon his Coming Home, receiv'd
'of the Gift of his moft Gracious Sove-
'reign and Mafter, the late King *James*
'the IId, a very Valuable Gold Chain and
'Medal, as an Evidence of his Favourable
'Acceptance of this Remarkable Service;
'befides a confiderable Prefent from the
'Honourable *Eaft-India* Company, out
'of their Grateful Senfe of his having fo
'faithfully and effectually difcharg'd the
'feveral important Trufts, committed by
'them to his Management.

'I *HENRY*, Earl of *Suffolk* and *Bin-*
'*don*, &c. One of the Lords of Her Ma-
'jefty's moft Honourable Privy Council,
'and Deputy (with the Royal Approbati-
'on) to his Grace, *Thomas* Duke of *Nor-*
'*folk*, Earl Marfhal, and Hereditary
'Marfhal of *England*, ferioufly weighing
'the

' the Premifes, do hereby therefore order
' and appoint you to make fuch Additions
' to the faid Coat, and Alteration in the
' Creft of the faid Sir *Thomas Grantham*,
' Knight, as may fitly perpetuate his Me-
' rit, and (after my Approbation) to af-
' fign the fame in ufual Form to him, and
' his Pofterity, to diftinguifh them ac-
' cordingly. Requiring you to take Care
' that my faid Approbation, together with
' thefe Prefents, and the Inftrument and
' Pattent for fuch Additions and Alterati-
' ons, be enter'd by the Regifter in the
' College of Arms. For all which this
' fhall be your fufficient Warrant. Given
' under my Hand and Seal, the   Day
' of   in the Tenth Year of the
' Reign of our Sovereign Lady *Anne*, by
' the Grace of God, Queen of *Great Bri-*
' *tain*, *France*, and *Ireland*, Defender of
' the Faith, &c. *Annoq; Domini*, 1711.

To Sir Henry St. George, *Kt. Garter,*
Principal King of Arms; and John
Vanbrugh, *Efq; Clarenceux, King*
of Arms.

I do

I *Do hereby upon Oath attest, that the Facts herein contain'd, relating to my Self, are true; And that the other Matters, here represented, are agreeable to the Informations, given by my Mother, and Others.*

Tho. Grantham.

Jurat. 10. Julij 1711.
  coram me,

  Jo. Meller.

F I N I S.